WISLEY HAND

CACTI

CLIVE INNES

LONDON
The Royal Horticultural Society
Reprinted 1980

Contents

CACTI

Introduction

Soon after the turn of the century the collection and cultivation of cacti gained considerable popularity, and this trend has continually developed year by year. In the early 1900's comparatively few species were readily available, and it is conceivable that the very lack of plant material encouraged the "cult"—for surely "cult" it is! As more and more species were discovered and introduced, increased enthusiasm became very apparent —an enthusiasm which has undoubtedly not yet reached its peak.

At the present time over 200 genera are represented in the family Cactaceae involving numerous species, varieties and forms, the majority of which are, to a greater or lesser degree, available in cultivation. Many specialist establishments have been founded to propagate, distribute and encourage interest in cacti. At the Holly Gate Botanical Collection in West Sussex, an extensive array of succulent plants has been assembled for reference and research purposes, embracing most known genera of cacti. Propagations from this Collection have found their way into countless public and private collections throughout the world.

Cacti, together with all succulent plants, are adaptable for many purposes, having the propensity for either home adornment or greenhouse culture and attraction—and in some instances are used as garden plants in more favoured areas of Britain. Remembering their real home—on one hand the harsh semi-arid expanses of North and South American deserts with all the natural problems which can be associated with such a habitat—and at the other extreme, the jungle homes of many well known and popular species where they grow epiphytically in company with orchids and bromeliads—this vast family is indeed unique.

Conservation is now widely recognised as a necessity and this would appear to apply particularly to cacti. In the name of progress and economic development whole regions of desert and jungle have, and are still being cleared of their natural plant populations to make space for food production, highways and townships. Perhaps to a lesser degree the indiscriminate collection of wild plants by man has helped to devastate further cactus habitats. Therefore with these conditions prevailing, conservation is a very important and urgent factor. Natural areas must be preserved where at all possible, and equally essential is the conservation of cacti in botanical collections, both public and private.

Cacti are "succulents" in the general sense of the word. There are perhaps a few exceptions whose structure does not merit the term "succu-

3

lent"—but these are very much in the minority. Their ability to store moisture and nourishment enables them to survive—they are used to privation and "plan" for it. Desert rainfall is sporadic and invariably fierce when it comes, even to the extent of causing temporary flooding of the flat open spaces. Due to the porous nature of the ground, the waters quickly subside—but during this period the plants have to take up and store nourishment until the next storm, perhaps many months or even years ahead. They have adjusted themselves fully to their environment. These facts must be constantly borne in mind when considering the best methods of cultivation—in many instances associating cultural requirements with natural habitat peculiarities.

In this book I hope that suitable guidance can be offered for better understanding of these many exotic and bizarre plants—to suggest guide-lines for their care and propagation—temperature, watering, positioning and other relevant aspects—and, what to expect from mature plants.

1. Geographical Distribution

All cacti are native to the New World. In many other parts of the tropical. and sub-tropical world certain species have become naturalised and quite mistakenly are considered native plants of their new home, such as in South Africa, Australia and southern Europe. There is evidence that a handful of cactus species have been encountered as wild plants in parts of East Africa and Madagascar—these being mainly epiphytic*. It has not been finally decided whether or not they are endemic to these parts or "escapes" which have gradually adjusted their appearance and perhaps habits to meet conditions prevailing in their immediate surroundings.

The cactus sphere extends from southern Canada through to many central, western and southern parts of the United States, Mexico, Central America, the West Indian Islands and all South American countries right down to the southernmost tip of Argentina. Many species, and for that matter genera, differ noticeably according to altitude—from sea-level to elevations of over 5000 m.

Mexico has the greatest concentration of cactus; here temperatures and humidity vary considerably—on the Baja California, the Pacific coastal areas enjoy a warm comfortable climate, whilst regions bordering the Gulf of California are frequently oppressively hot. These conditions provide the habitat of some of the more uncommon *Echinocereus* and *Opuntia* species, likewise *Machaeorcereus*, the Creeping Devil, a plant unknown elsewhere. On the mainland in Sonora and Sinaloa are many different *Mammillaria*, *Echinocereus* and *Ferocactus* together with occasional colonies of rarer genera such as *Wilcoxia*, *Neovansia* and *Peniocereus*. Perhaps the most dominating plants found here are *Lemaire-*

*Epiphyte = a plant growing on another but not parasitic.

4

ocereus and *Pachycereus* which, with *Carnegia gigantea,* the huge saguaro, also a native of Arizona, are truly spectacular. From Chihuahua and Coahuila southwards are to be seen *Astrophytum, Ariocarpus, Thelocactus, Hamatocactus* and *Lophophora.* The choice *Mammillaria plumosa* (see Fig. 1) is located at altitudes of 2000 m. Further south, on limestone cliffs in Hidalgo is the habitat of *Cephalocereus senilis,* one of the most distinctive Mexican cacti. Below Mexico City where are situated the moist tropical forest zones of Chiapas—these extending through to Guatemala, Honduras and Costa Rica—the scene changes, and the first evidence of epiphytic cacti—*Epiphyllum, Hylocereus, Disocactus, Selenicereus* and *Rhipsalis* can be observed. Notwithstanding this change, on the more barren mountain slopes, often in close proximity to the forest are further species of *Opuntia* and columnar *Cereus* and some of the sprawling, trailing *Acanthocereus, Nyctocereus* and the like.

Many parts of South America and the West Indies have dense rain forest areas. Rare plants such as *Strophocactus wittii* can be discovered in the Amazon forests—whilst typical jungle cacti—*Rhipsalis, Zygocactus, Schlumbergera, Epiphyllum* and *Epiphyllanthus*—are native of Brazil, some genera also being represented in Peru, Chile and Ecuador. The West Indies have a number of isolated examples of epiphytic cacti—mainly *Rhipsalis, Hylocereus, Selenicereus* and *Epiphyllum.*

South America has been the scene of many important and extensive

Fig. 1. *Mammillaria plumosa*

5

expeditions since 1950, particularly in Ecuador, Peru, Chile and Southern Brazil. Species of *Oroya*, *Borzicactus*, *Neoporteria* and *Islaya* from Peru have been discovered and introduced into cultivation in more recent years, adding to the already known cacti of *Espostoa*, *Melocactus*, *Tephrocactus*, a miniature group of the Opuntieae, and many more. Ecuador is well represented by species of *Trichocereus*, *Armatocereus* and the more columnar *Borzicactus*.

Chile has almost a monopoly of certain genera—*Copiapoa*, *Horridocactus*, *Reicheocactus*, *Eulychnia* and *Neowerdermannia* to mention but a few—these occurring at varying elevations from the flat coastal plains to some of the higher rocky slopes of the Andes. The totally encompassed Bolivia is the home of *Lobivia*—an anagram of Bolivia—*Gymnocalycium*, *Rebutia*, *Cleistocactus*, *Sulcorebutia*, *Quiabentia* and others. Paraguay and Brazil share a number of genera, *Parodia*, *Notocactus*, *Echinopsis*, *Melocactus*, *Discocactus* and more besides. Southern Brazil has provided some of the most exciting new discoveries of cacti, *Discocactus horstii*, a charming miniature; species of a fairly new genus, *Uebelmannia*; *Buiningia* and *Coleocephalocereus*, all within these groups having most outstanding and distinctive characteristics.

Northern Argentina, together with Uruguay, is the habitat of *Oreocereus*, *Gymnocalycium*, *Chamaecereus*, *Cleistocactus*, *Notocactus* and *Pfeiffera*. On the high mountain slopes of Patagonia in more southerly Argentina are *Maihuenia*, a genus rarely encountered in cultivation—almost an 'alpine' cactus—related to *Opuntia*. It might be interesting to note at this stage that no genus has more representation than *Opuntia*—being found continuously from southern Canada to southern Argentina.

Just a brief mention of two important cactus habitats. The West Indies have comparatively few genera of this family—possibly *Melocactus* is the most widely distributed and species often vary considerably from one island to the other. Cuba would appear to have the greatest representation —certainly more different species of *Melocactus* are found there, also *Dendrocereus*, *Harrisia* and *Leptocereus*.

The Galapagos Islands have for many years been a plant sanctuary and any species from these islands are considered uncommon. Two genera are totally confined to these parts—*Jasminocereus* and *Brachycereus*—also, once again, *Opuntia*, which from these islands are possibly among the most attractive of this vast genus.

2. Characteristics

All cacti are dicotyledons—that is to say, they have two seed leaves when they germinate, and all are perennial. Therefore, not being annuals or biennials, maturity to the flowering stage is not usually reached in one growing season—a much longer period is common—although there are exceptions.

The Cactaceae as a family are provided with many distinguishing features which set them apart from any other form of plant life. The most prominent characteristic is the areole, a round or elongated cushion of 'felt' or hair and this is apparent to a greater or lesser degree on the plant stems or bodies. The areole actually incorporates two growing points—the upper one produces the flower buds and 'branches' (if the species is one which offsets or 'branches'), and spines (if the species has spination) develop from the lower one. With certain genera these two growing points are set well apart—this is particularly evident with *Mammillaria*—but generally they are closely set together so as to make them appear almost united. In the case of some epiphytic genera—e.g. *Epiphyllum*, *Schlumbergera*—the areoles are difficult to locate, being very minute.

The cephalium is a woolly cap formed at the growing point of certain cacti of flowering size, which increases in size annually. It comprises densely-packed woolly areoles and sometimes bristles (not spines) and bears the flowers.

Most epiphytic cacti are readily distinguishable—the flattish stem growth being very leaf-like. *Epiphyllum*, *Disocactus*, *Nopalxochia* and a few others come into this category, and a few species have either deep or shallow crenations along the margins. With the genus *Schlumbergera* the leaf-like segments are oblong or rounded with slightly discernible crenated edges, or 'toothed' segments with *Zygocactus*, and these pointed crenations are most apparent.

Other epiphytic types have rather different stem features. *Hylocereus*, which includes some species with the largest flowers in the Cactaceae, are climbing, clambering plants, generally with triangular shaped stems with woody margins and few stumpy hard spines. In all species, aerial roots develop, sparsely, along the stems and at the constructions (points which denote where new growth starts). *Selenicereus*, also with large nocturnal flowers, is likewise a climber and generally provided with many aerial roots. The elongated stems possess distinctive rib formation, some with prominent projections at intervals along the ribs. New growth can be 3, 4, 5 or 6 sided, and this is very apparent, but with maturity, stems become almost roundish.

Of all epiphytic cacti, the most difficult to determine—and controversial —are *Rhipsalis*, and *Lepismium* and others of related genera. Botanically *Lepismium* are identified because of a sunken ovary in the stem margin. The stem growth varies greatly, often 3-angled with a purplish red appearance, slightly undulating. Others have rib-like formations or link-stems developing into whorls. All have very pronounced areoles and generally few, if any, spines but aerial roots are always in evidence. All species of *Rhipsalis* have fairly small, sometimes insignificant, flowers. Stems are usually spineless although a few have soft bristles or hairs which can disappear with age. Without exception they are of pendent habit with

7

mostly elongated stems and branches, but differing tremendously in form. Long slender pencil-shaped stems are typical of many, either in short sections or long growths to 3 feet (1 m.) or more in length. Others have angular stems, pronouncedly triangular or with 5–7 distinct ribs. A few have leaf-like sections similar to *Epiphyllum* or *Schlumbergera* with 'leaves' often crenated, occasionally with undulating margins. All species have aerial roots, and areoles more or less obvious.

Those comprising the desert or semi-desert *Cerei* are fairly readily recognisable, being in the main columnar plants. The erect species are possibly in the majority—although to give an overall characteristic to include all species would be impossible. Some are very heavily ribbed and spined, others only moderately so. A large number are night flowering, but not all. Some genera are of prostrate habit as with *Machaeocereus* which in nature trails many metres in length, and is viciously spined. *Heliocereus*, the Sun Cactus, is mainly 3 to 4 angled, frequently semi-pendent with startling orange, white or rich crimson flowers. Some species of this genus have been used to cross-pollinate with *Epiphyllums* to produce some of the exotic cultivars now available.

Mammillaria is one of the most popular and important genera—comprising a great number of diverse species which produce flowers of white through to rich purplish red. Some are caespitose, others of simple form—spination is generally dense with central and radial spines very apparent. The actual ribs are not so noticeable, the body of the plants being set with tubercles, mostly spirally arranged, without grooves. Flowers are borne in the axils of the tubercles from the upper part of the areole, always on the side of the plant—never terminal—frequently

Fig. 2.
A collection
of Mammillaria
species.

forming a complete circle around the upper part of the plant body.

Opuntieae include many genera, some with pad-shaped sections, others cylindrical in stem form. Some genera consist of plants with low growing habit, although once again the stems and branches consist of small, somewhat stunted, oval, round or elongated segments. The areoles of all have glochids—small barbed bristles or hairs in clusters—a peculiarity of the family. Glochids are capable of causing irritation to the skin of the careless or unwary—they are so easily broken off.

The majority of cacti do not possess leaves. Some species of *Opuntia* and *Cereus* have small fleshy leaves on new growth, but generally these soon drop off and rarely persist. The exception is found only with *Pereskia* which bear non-succulent leaves, invariably deciduous. Plants are of bushy, semi-erect or clambering habit and have large aeroles and long spines. Flowers are among the most attractive of the Cactaceae—somewhat rose-like, and coloured cream, yellow or magenta.

Only few notable exceptions among desert cacti are totally or partially spineless, or are replaced by hairs or bristles. In particular these features apply to *Ariocarpus*, *Aztekium*, *Lophophora* and certain species of *Astrophytum* and *Borzicactus*. Spines are certainly a very important characteristic, perhaps to the very knowledgeable a guide-line to the identification of a genus—maybe species!

The majority of the barrel-shaped or globular cacti—*Ferocactus*, *Echinocactus*, *Parodia*, *Notocactus*, *Echinopsis* have very decided symmetrical ribs—sometimes completely vertical, others spirally arranged. These may be widely spaced or set quite close together, so close—and so densely covered with spines and hairs—that with some species of *Parodia* and *Notocactus* it is well-nigh impossible to appreciate the rib formation. Flowers are, of course, the greatest feature of all—cactus or any other exotic plant family. All cacti do flower—a few, very few, have small uninteresting flowers—but by far the majority produce beautiful blooms, some to 8 inches (20 cm.) or more in diameter. Almost every colour is represented, with the exception of blue—many are very fragrant. Flowering can be either diurnal or nocturnal—and usually the night flowerers have the advantage of being heavily scented. Nocturnal flowers only open for one night, generally beginning to display themselves in late afternoon or evening and closing and withering soon after sunrise or during the early hours of the morning. Diurnal flowers open for a number of days in succession—some as many as four of five days. Unfortunately there are a number of exceptions, but plants with short-lived flowers are sometimes compensated by having many flowers appearing in succession over a period of many weeks, or even months.

The aspect of fruits and seeds is too complicated a subject to mention in detail in this booklet, but pertinent and relevant mention will be made later when considering species in more detail.

9

3. Guide to Cultivation

In the greenhouse

In most parts of the northern hemisphere the greenhouse serves as the most convenient and trustworthy method of growing exotics—and cacti certainly fall within this category. A few brief suggestions and warnings regarding the greenhouse:

(*a*) It must be sound, strong, and weatherproof.

(*b*) Drips from a leaking roof can cause much damage to the plants.

(*c*) Draughts are equally dangerous and should be stopped.

(*d*) Ventilation should be planned to give the best air circulation as needed—to stimulate plant growth and discourage stagnation.

(*e*) Good light is the main natural requirement of cacti—not necessarily full sun! Maintain this by providing a maximum glass area which should be kept clean.

(*f*) Some form of shading can be beneficial during excessive summer heat when the sun is at its height. Heating is a matter of choice, only beware of apparatus which gives off injurious fumes. Unless really tropical species are being cultivated, a minimum temperature of 8° to 10°C (46–50°F) is ample. However, when housing some of the supposedly temperamental cacti, such as species of *Melocactus* and *Discocactus*, the temperature must not fall below 15°C (59°F) or even higher.

If the greenhouse is to grow a mixed selection of semi-desert and epiphytic cacti—then some sort of segregation is essential. Epiphytes, which come from forests, do not require full sunlight. Many may conveniently be placed under the bench, but emphasis must be placed upon the necessity of avoiding too bright a situation. For all cacti within this category, good shading should be installed, although it may not be needed during the winter months.

Watering is very important—although with regard to this it is advisable to know your plants! Determine whether they are winter or summer growing and flowering, then water accordingly—not forgetting a favourable temperature for those that are winter growers.

When to water?—when the soil is dry, water well and soak thoroughly —then wait until the soil is dry again before repeating. With most of the desert cacti watering can be totally withheld from early November to March —although with some species restricted watering can prove advantageous. Water can safely be applied from overhead, but do not give it in the heat of the day. Early in the morning is the best time, before the sun rises too high—otherwise as late in the evening as possible when temperatures have dropped and plants are cooler. Do not leave cactus standing in water— complete and constant drainage is most essential and water-logging can be calamitous. Equally dangerous are small 'teaspoonfuls' of water each

10

day or so—plants must be left to use up their nourishment. It is just a matter of keeping in mind the periods of drought and sudden seasonal rainstorms common to cactus habitats.

Soil is possibly the most discussed aspect of cultivation. What suits and satisfies one enthusiast does not necessarily meet the ideas of another. The inclusion of grit or sharp sand in the soil mix cannot be too strongly recommended. The mixture *must* be porous to enable aeration to play its part. Nutrients should be incorporated into the mixture and should later be maintained by feeding in order to encourage and sustain growth and flowering. Many good composts are now commercially prepared and available from garden shops. Soilless composts have gained considerable popularity, and these are easily adapted for cacti when 30% or more of the bulk consists of small, sharp, washed grit. Most soilless composts are manufactured with the appropriate nutrients added, but these may only last for a limited period of weeks or months depending upon the absorption of the plant.

Many other branded soil-based composts can give equally good results. The best known is perhaps the John Innes series and these are satisfactory, although even with these it may be necessary to add more grit.

It is with a certain hesitation that a 'do-it-yourself' compost is mentioned, mainly because really good loam is now very difficult to obtain. However, if a good loam that is totally uncontaminated can be procured, the following will make a good mixture:

1 part good, sterilised loam;
1 part well sifted, decomposed leafmould;
1 part sharp, gritty, washed sand;

plus a sprinkling of slow release fertilizer (such as Enmag). It is simple, but efficient—and, if really good decomposed cow manure can be included in moderate quantity, even better results may be expected. Many growers also include charcoal chippings in soil mixture, this helping to offset the problem of souring the soil.

Feeding of cacti has been mentioned very briefly earlier; only those growing well with an efficient root system, will absorb nutrients, and a quick reaction is generally the case. Plants which look dehydrated or out-of-form are best removed from their pots and carefully examined for pest or rot. Clean or cut to clear out the problem, then re-establish the plants before starting to feed them again.

Fertilizers are numerous, but very few have been prepared specifically for cactus growing. Most contain nitrogen and potash in varying proportions, and this may be very good. It is wise to try to use fertilizers containing the essential trace elements of iron, magnesium, manganese, copper, boron and molybdenum—all of which play a part in producing the sort of plant to which the enthusiast aspires! The type of container to use is a matter of opinion—plastic or clay. What matters is that the

11

technique of watering with each is different—clay pots dry out more quickly, whilst the soil in a plastic pot can remain moist for a much longer period. If the two are kept side-by-side, and given the same treatment, one or other will suffer—and this is what is really meant by **care**. Cacti do not thrive on neglect—they may survive, but not for long if the neglect continues, and eventually there will be no plant at all.

Cacti in the home

Cacti have long flourished as house plants—many are well known —and as various seasons of the year come around, we see many species of Christmas cactus, Easter cactus, and an increasing number of epiphyllums, adorning multitudes of homes. In fact, cacti make excellent house plants, and usually prove easy to grow.

Most desert plants—especially those of compact growth—adapt readily to conditions in houses and these include many species which flower easily and have most attractive spination. These are possibly most suitable for growing in a container, making bowl gardens. A number of such cacti planted carefully can be a pleasure for many years.

The selection is vast, and later in this book, mention will be made of those most suitable for this purpose. The main essential is the preparation of the container. Most bowls are too shallow, and care should be taken to select one which is at least 4 inches (10 cm.) deep—the deeper the better. Another disadvantage with some containers is that there are no drainage holes, and this can cause problems. It is therefore very necessary to crock the base well—using broken pieces of clay pots, or medium sized washed gravel is recommended—and this should be to a depth of about 4 inches (9 cm). Charcoal chippings can be included with the crocking, helping to maintain the sweetness of the compost.

Planting is best done when the soil is not quite dry, then left to settle and establish for a week or two in a light, airy position. Then firm around the plants, and water very carefully. The crocking will act as a reservoir, but it must not become a miniature pond. Excess water—or water applied too often—will rot the roots and cause irreparable damage. The use of a hydrometer is recommended for these growing conditions. Allowing for a resting period applies equally in the home as in the greenhouse—but if a very high temperature is kept indoors, then occasional moderate watering can safely be given. Fertilizer is equally essential in home culture. Soil is less likely to be changed in bowl gardens than when plants are in pots, which is all the more reason for regular feeding during the growing season, about every 10–14 days is sufficient, and then only in small quantities.

As mentioned earlier, epiphyllums are excellent examples of good house plants. These have been popular for well over a 100 years—for many years only *Epiphyllum* 'Ackermannii' was available, and as this multiplied readily by cuttings it soon had a wide distribution. Many hundreds of different cultivars are now on the market—the majority are well suited for home culture, producing their large exotic blooms from March through to late June or even July. They are less harmed by over-watering than many other cacti—and given just ordinary care will thrive for years on end. Among some of the finest and outstanding cultivars are the following and these can be recommended for home culture:

'Alba Superbus', large white with fragrant flowers.
'Midnight', large flower, dark red and purple.
'Space Rocket', one of the largest of flowers, purple, lavender and magenta.
'Reward', generally considered to be one of the best yellow flowering varieties.
'Royal Token', rich orange and red.
'Red Velvet', sheen red.
'Professor Ebert', compact plant, lilac pink.
'Pink Nymph', beautiful flesh pink.
'Autumn', coral pink.
'Primrose', a more dwarf plant with pale yellow flowers.
'Jaybee', bright pink with pronounced deeper midrib of almost purple.

There are many more than these, and specialist nurseries can supply lists and information.

Other popular cacti which have an especially seasonal appeal are species and cultivars of *Schlumbergera* and *Zygocactus*. The typical Christmas cactus with its bright magenta flowers is actually a cultivar of many years standing, now botanically known as *Schlumbergera* 'Bridgesii'. In recent years a number of cultivars have found their way into homes throughout Europe—plants with white, pink, pale orange, orange-red and deep magenta flowers. All of these have zygomorphic flowers and might well be considered hybrids of *Zygocactus*—but the latest botanic nomenclature has merged these two genera—so they are known commercially as *Schlumbergera*. During the spring months a number of different Easter cactus produce their flowers in abundance. These too are remarkably good and adaptable house plants, giving flowers for many weeks on end. Botanically known as *Rhipsalidopsis gaertneri*—these have regular flowers, as does also the lilac form 'Elektra'. With all these epiphytic species, it is unnecessary to dry the soil completely at any time, but wetness must be avoided, just maintaining a slightly moist condition and fertilizing regularly, especially throughout the growing and flowering seasons.

4. Propagation

The propagation of cacti is not difficult, and there are many ways whereby plants can be increased at relatively little cost.

The advantages of raising cacti from seed are threefold—firstly, it is economical; secondly, seedlings so raised usually develop true to type and with care can make good specimen plants; and thirdly, plants adapt themselves to the conditions where they are to be grown right from the beginning, and this can be a great advantage. Apart from any other consideration, it can prove stimulating and satisfying in later years to have in your possession spectacular plants of your own raising.

Seeds are fairly easy to procure—many excellent seed firms offer mixtures, and this can prove useful for the beginner, the only snag being that such packets contain seeds of various species, the seeds more often than not being of considerably different sizes. For the advanced collector, numerous species of cacti seed are obtainable from specialist firms at moderate prices—and this affords the satisfaction of knowing precisely what you are sowing, how to deal with them, and what eventually to expect. With only rare exceptions seeds are viable for two years or more —but it is certainly best to try and obtain fresh seeds, for easier and quicker germination.

Commercially prepared seed composts are readily available and in general these can be recommended. When preparing the container it is necessary to cover the base with very gravelly soil so as to give good drainage, but be sure this is sterilized. Then fill the container with seed compost to within about ½ in. (1·5 cm) of the top, firm well to make a level surface—this is important, as it prevents any overhead watering at a later date from collecting in one place. Seeds vary tremendously in size, ranging from 2 mm. or more in diameter to almost dust-like; this is where mixed packets of seeds can prove a problem. Seeds should be spread evenly over the surface of the compost, then covered lightly to about the depth of the diameter of the seed sown. In the case of really dust-like seeds, they can be safely left uncovered—they very soon find their 'anchor'. Many species will germinate in a matter of days, whilst others, and there are several of them, may take months before they germinate. After sowing the seeds, place the container (but do not submerge it) in tepid water until the whole, right to the surface, is thoroughly moistened. Take it out, allow to drain for a while, then cover with glass or/and paper, place in a propagator or in a place away from direct sunlight and maintain a temperature of about 22°C (71·5°F) throughout the period of germination. Never allow the compost to dry out, but beware of undue wetness as this can rot the seeds and certainly the seedlings. Humidity is a good thing, but not in excess—if moisture condenses too much on the covering glass this indicates that the humidity is too high. In this case, wipe away the condensation and keep the glass slightly lifted to give more ventilation. When germination has taken place, seedlings should be gradually acclimatized to being plants—giving them more and more light as they develop, and good but careful ventilation. Seed sowing is best done early in the year so long as a regular temperature can be maintained—and seedlings should be kept growing for a period of at least nine months, preferably through the following winter and into the next normal growing period. The one great danger to seedlings in the early weeks is damping-off, and prevention is better than cure. Cheshunt compound, captan, or zineb are recommended preventatives. Mix any of these with water and lightly spray over the seedlings at the first watering following germination —it will prevent many disappointments later.

Don't be too eager to prick out seedlings; wait until they are of sufficient size to be handled easily and after they have taken on something of the appearance of the parent plant. Overcrowding is not necessarily harmful if they are left undisturbed for quite a long while.

Many species can be propagated by cuttings—this can be either by deliberate severing of the stem sections, or by the removal of pads in the case of *Opuntia* or offsets as with species of *Echinopsis, Mammillaria* and other similarly grouping plants. It must not be a 'breaking off, putting in' process—it is basically fairly easy, but nevertheless requires thought and care. A clean sharp knife should be used when making the cuts—the cuttings should then be allowed to callus thoroughly (by exposing the cut surface to the air for several days) before setting firmly in slightly moist, very gritty soil—placed in a warm shady position until rooting has taken place. Only take cuttings in warm settled weather—never give much water, although occasional spraying overhead can prove useful to avoid dehydration. When removed offsets already have roots, they can safely be potted and treated as normal plants. Species of *Epiphyllum* and other kindred genera require slightly different attention. Stems of *Epiphyllum* can be cut into a number of pieces and each will be capable of producing a plant—cuts should be clean and deliberate—from an areole on one side to an areole on the other. Single or multiple sections can be removed from *Zygocactus* or *Schlumbergera* for propagation purposes—in all cases make sure the cuts have dried thoroughly before setting. A somewhat higher humidity than provided for desert plants can hasten rooting. The compost can be more moist, but not too much so—a temperature of 22°C (71.5°F) regularly maintained will encourage rapid root growth, and new stem growth will be only a matter of weeks.

Grafting is less frequently used as a method of propagation. It consists of a stem cutting, called the scion, being joined to the stem of another growing plant, called the stock. This operation is done without either cut drying, the principle being literally to fuse the two together. Grafting

15

should not be done for the sake of grafting—if a plant grows well on its own roots, it is purposeless to graft. Grafting is mainly for propagating species inclined to be temperamental or especially slow growing on their own roots. The best time to graft is the early summer—at this time active growth is apparent and this effectively helps the union. There are varied methods of grafting—the most usual and easy is the flat graft which is simply to cut straight across both scion and stock with reasonably compatible cut surfaces, bevelling the edges to avoid the scion being forced off as the edges dry out. By the careful use of a rubber band, the two can be securely held together until they have united. Another method is the cleft graft, and this is generally used for more slender plants like the Christmas cactus. A V-shaped cut is made in the stock, the scion is cut to a wedge shape and inserted into the stock. These can be held together by soft and flexible, but thin, string or very carefully placed rubber bands. Sometimes it is wise to insert a cactus spine right through from side to side to prevent the scion slipping out of the cleft. Other methods are available, but the two mentioned are most popular.

Left: A cleft graft, held in place with a cactus spine.
Right: A flat graft   //// = *Stock*

   Care must be taken to select the best stock for grafting. Most globular species take readily to *Trichocereus*, *Echinopsis* or *Harrisia* stock. Many miniature cacti such as *Blossfeldia*, a very slow-growing species, can be united to *Pereskia* or *Pereskiopsis* stock. Usually *Schlumbergera*, *Zygocactus* and certain epiphytic species of slow-growing or rather temperamental habit can be safely grafted to *Selenicereus* or *Pereskia*. As the scion is very slender with such plants, only the skin of the portion to be inserted should carefully be removed and immediately inserted into the cleft and held in position as suggested above.

Recent years have seen the introduction and propagation of plants without chlorophyll. Chlorophyll produces the green colouring in a plant, and the absence of it can lead to many peculiarities in seedlings. In a sense these might be considered 'freaks'—small seedlings with red, yellow or white plant bodies that have germinated and fed on the cotyledon and would normally have died with the cotyledon. However, the idea of saving these little seedlings was developed in Japan—and grafting them to species of *Trichocereus* or *Hylocereus* has enabled them to grow more or less to maturity. The 'red-knobs' and 'yellow-knobs', which are seen offered are the result of this culture. Whether or not such plants attract us is immaterial—the fact is that grafting has made this possible.

Abnormal growths occur in some genera and are usually linked with genetic disturbances in the plants. In the Cactaceae these are referred to as cristate (crested) or monstrose forms. These peculiarities are brought about by the multiplication of the grow-

ing points. With cristates a fan-shaped growth develops and often becomes wavy and twisted. Monstrose growths are produced by the continued multiplication of the growing points, these being a mass of many miniature shoots. This fasciation can occur from seedling stage and throughout any period of the plant's life. It is, however, possible for such peculiarities to revert to normal, and if left growing on their own roots, this could be likely to happen. To maintain the attraction of these abnormalities, the cristate or monstrose sections are grafted on to suitable stock. The same process suggested for grafting true forms, equally applies here—but be sure to select appropriate stock as both cristates and monstrose forms can grow large and impressive.

Fig. 3. Notocactus Scopa Cristate.

17

5. Pests and Diseases

No cacti are immune from pests, but precautions can be taken to restrict their ill-effects upon our plants. Diseases, on the other hand, are often due to negligence such as over-watering or bruising—and these may cause immeasurable harm to the plant body and perhaps more so to the root system. Some cacti are sensitive to insecticides but the risk of spray damage can be reduced by applying the insecticide in cool cloudy weather and not when the roots are dry. Here are given some of the most common problems affecting cacti.

A. PESTS

Mealy-bug. Has the appearance of a very small woodlouse, covered with a white fibrous substance. The eggs are contained within the white tufts which are usually close to the bug. Mild infestations can be dealt with by applying, with a small paint-brush, a mix of 1 part nicotine to 3 parts methylated spirit. Alternatively, use malathion diluted as prescribed on the bottle, or a systemic insecticide.

Root mealybugs are smaller than mealybugs and suck sap from the roots. Heavy infestations cause poor growth and examination of the roots should reveal the pests, often surrounded by white waxy powder on roots and soil particles. The soil can be gently washed from the roots which are then dipped in spray-strength malathion before repotting in fresh soil. Systemic insecticides watered on the soil will help to control attacks when repotting is inconvenient.

Red Spider Mite. Reddish orange in colour, very minute in size, almost like dust. They colonise and become surrounded by very fine webs. The pest sucks the sap and gradually the plant body becomes brownish and disfigured. The cause is generally too dry a condition or bad ventilation. The pests appear to dislike a humid atmosphere—so if this can be produced, together with good ventilation, at least their presence will not be encouraged. Systemic insecticides and malathion are available to deal with this pest.

White Fly. A dangerous and persistent pest which does not attack cacti too much. They are nevertheless difficult to eradicate—and BHC 'smokes' for use in greenhouses or sprays containing pyrethrum, bioresmethrin or resmethrin are available for this purpose.

Scale insects are sap feeding pests with a shell-like covering over their bodies, rather like a limpet, brown or greyish-brown, about 1/12–1/6 in. (2–4 mm) across. Eggs are laid under the cover of the scale and these hatch into larvae which crawl about looking for a suitable feeding place, when they become immobile for the rest of their lives. Sprays containing malathion or a systemic insecticide are effective, especially if applied when the young scales are hatching.

Sciarid Fly. This is most frequently associated with peat-based composts or soils with a high degree of non-decomposed humus included in a soil mix. These are minute grey flies which lay their eggs in the soil and the small white grubs eat the roots of seedlings and mature plants. Control by watering the plants with spray-strength malathion.

Many other pests such as slugs and snails (control by methiocarb or metaldehyde slug pellets), ants and woodlice (control by BHC dust) can also attack cacti, at times.

B. DISEASES

Black-rot. A disease which primarily attacks epiphytic cacti, the blackening of the stem is usually at soil level or just below, supposedly caused by the bacteria entering the plant body and turning the tissues black and soft. The diseased area can be cut out, but the operation must be done very thoroughly or the trouble will re-occur. It has also been suggested that the complaint has an association with too high a nitrogen content in the soil. Whatever the reason, black rot occurs too often and undoubtedly a copper-based fungicide will help to prevent it taking control.

Damping-off. This is generally only a seedling problem. A good fungicide will prove the only remedy—captan, Cheshunt compound or zineb can be recommended.

Rust. This is not a disease but is mainly due to water being retained on the exposed body of the plant.

It must be borne in mind that many troubles can be avoided if careful watch is kept. When a plant ceases to grow and shows signs of shrivelling, the cause may be over or under-watering; under-potting or perhaps the souring of the soil. In the latter case the cause is emphasised by the appearance of algae or greenish moss on the soil surface. Control is really a matter of care—always try to avoid problems of your own making or carelessness, and you will be rewarded with attractive, healthy plants.

Warning.

Mention has been made of insecticides and fungicides and it should be remembered that such chemicals may be highly poisonous. Be careful in handling—give the required dosage—and if protective clothing, such as gloves, has been advised—then act accordingly. Above all, keep such commodities well away from the reach of children and pets.

6. Directory of Cacti

This record is not intended to be comprehensive, certainly not of species and not even all-embracing of the genera. A selection has been prepared of those most likely to be encountered in nurseries and garden shops, and species which are very desirable to the connoisseur but not difficult to grow. Consideration has also been given to the particularly attractive characteristics of shape and colour, ready adaption to greenhouse or home culture and readiness to flower.

Aporocactus (Mexico)

Trailing plants with long stems, sometimes to 3 feet (1 m). Generally considered epiphytic even to developing aerial roots. Some species have been hybridised with other genera, especially *Epiphyllum*, resulting in many beautiful cultivars of easy culture—the inter-generic title being × *Aporophyllum*.

A. flagelliformis, the well-known rat's tail cactus. Slender stems, 10–12 ribs, soft spines and bright crimson, zygomorphic, flowers lasting for several days. Light position essential but not full sun. Fairly acid soil for best results.

A. leptophis is a rare epiphyte having 7–8 ribs and reddish flowers with lilac shading. Spines are numerous and quite stiff.

A. mallisonii is actually a hybrid between *Heliocereus speciosus* and *A. flagelliformis* proving very popular for years past. Has thick pendent stems, well spined and deep scarlet flowers Very free flowering.

Arequipa (Chile and Peru)

Somewhat globular plants and now considered part of the genus *Borzicactus*.

A. leucotricha has closely set areoles with many spines and red flowers on a long slender tube. Only a few species are included in the genus, all having very similar characteristics.

Ariocarpus (Mexico and Texas)

Low growing, spineless plants with broad somewhat triangular tubercles, sometimes called 'living rock'. Full sun, sandy soil, with lime added and careful watering essential. Plants have long tuber-like roots.

A. fissuratus. One of the largest of the genus, to about 8 in. (20 cm) diameter. Tubercles warty and greyish. Flowers in late summer from centre of plant, purplish pink.

A. retusus has a flattened or depressed surface about 5–6 in. (12–15 cm) diameter, horny tubercles, greyish, tending to overlap one another. Flowers white, appearing from the axils of the young tubercles at the crown.

Arrojadoa (Brazil)

Long slender cylindrical-stemmed plants with apical pseudocephalium from which flowers develop. New growth continues through the cephalium to form another apical cephalium for future flowering—this continuing, to produce a stem ringed periodically with thick clustered bristly hairs.

A. canudosensis. An erect plant to 3 feet (1 m) high with brown and white bristly cephalium. A fairly recent introduction with tubular, pinkish green flowers. A connoisseur's plant.

A. rhodantha is of rather clambering habit, dark green body with slender spines. Flowers from apex, about an inch (3 cm) long, pink.

Astrophytum (Mexico)

A popular and fascinating genus, each species having unique characteristics—some species have no spines. They accept moderate watering

20

throughout growing season. but the soil must be porous with lime added.
A. asterias, commonly called the bishops' mitre, being spineless and very similar to a de-spined sea urchin in appearance. Flowers yellow with the centre slightly flushed reddish.

A. capricorne has long twisted blackish brown spines set on broadly spaced ribs. Flowers yellow.

A. ornatum is another of the genus with spines. It has a number of forms with varying body colourings, green, white, grey or partially mottled. Ribs are widely spaced, fluted, with yellow flowers, centred red.

A. myriostigma—well known as the bishop's cap—somewhat rounded in shape, becoming semi-columnar with age. Generally only 3–5 ribs, rarely more, covered with white woolly scales. There are a number of varietal forms each with distinctive characteristics. Flower yellow.

Blossfeldia (Argentina)
Comprising some of the most miniature species within the Cactaceae. Mostly multiheaded and somewhat difficult on their own roots, therefore grafting is advisable.

B. liliputana is a flattish cylindrical plant, greyish green with minute

Fig. 4.
Astrophytum
species.

21

greyish woolly areoles, and totally spineless. Whitish pink flowers develop towards the apex.

Borzicactus (Ecuador, Peru, etc.)
A genus which has enveloped many others—*Matucana, Submatucana, Oroya, Arequipa, Akersia,* etc. A cause for much research on both sides of the Atlantic, and controversy and consternation by those who have to accept the findings. There are many plant forms, but the flowers are reasonably similar.
B. aurantiacus (*Submatucana aurantiaca*) is a beautiful species from Peru with orange-red flowers from the crown of the plant.
B. auriespinus (*Hildewinteria auriespina*) is of pendent habit having long dense spines, white with brown tips. Flowers orange-red on long slender tube.
B. haynei (*Matucana haynei*), also from Peru, is a globular species with cylindrical stems of golden yellow, this effect being created by the masses of golden spines. Flowers orange.

Buiningia (Brazil)
A rare and interesting genus with short cylindrical stems and pseudo-cephalium gradually covering nearly one side of the plant body.
B. brevicylindrica has pronounced areoles and many spines, yellowish becoming grey. Golden-yellow bristles of cephalium become black with age. Flowers small, yellowish green.

Cephalocereus (Mexico)
A large genus which has been divided and reduced to only a few species. Among the most distinctive of the columnar cacti, and reasonably easy in cultivation but requiring complete dryness in winter.
C. senilis, Old Man Cactus. Is tall growing and elegant, covered with dense long white hairs that almost completely envelop the stems. Flowers are rose-pink, about 2 in. (5 cm) long. Mature plants of about 18 ft. (6 m) high will have developed pseudocephaliums.

Cereus (South America, West Indies)
Well known and popular plants with tall, stately and much branched stems. All are nocturnal flowering and generally fragrant. A large genus of easy culture.
C. peruvianus and its monstrose form are well known. Stems are dark green with up to 9 broad ribs with brown-black spines. Large white flowers. Used for grafting stock.
C. hexagonus has 6 ribs, rather thin, with small felted areoles, short spines and very large scented white flowers.

Chamaecereus (Argentina)
A popular genus since its inception, but now officially transferred to the genus *Lobivia*—although the change will not be readily accepted by most collectors.

Fig. 5. (*left*
Copiapoa
cinerea.

Fig. 6. (*right*)
Cephalocereus
senilis.
"*The Old Man*
Cactus"

23

C. silvestrii, the peanut cactus, has strong, rapid growth with a series of blunt but small cylindrical stems looking like peanuts. Short spines and bristles are numerous, and bright red flowers develop easily in both greenhouse and home if kept well watered in warm weather and given a bright position.

Cleistocactus (South America)

Plants with erect or clambering habit. Flowers are unusual, being mostly tubular, the tip being barely open with only the stamens and style protruding. Of easy culture.

C. strausii is the best known of the genus with erect white bristly stems and long red tubular flowers along the length of the stems.

C. wendlandiorum—one of the most uncommon species from western Argentina, having stout stems with short golden-yellow spines and deep orange flowers.

Copiapoa (Chile)

Distinctive globular plants with small flowers, much sought after by collectors. In general they make excellent greenhouse plants, and accept quite cold conditions.

C. cinerea has a whitish grey body with dense white wool in the crown and about 18 broad ribs with closely set areoles and small black spines. Flowers are yellow.

C. krainziana is an exceptional plant with longish white hair-like bristles and golden spines, rather uncommon in cultivation.

Coryphantha (Mexico, Texas, Arizona and California)

A large genus of globular plants, with tubercles bearing stiff spines. Flowers usually in the crown of the plant. Very porous soil necessary, and lime added is an advantage. All require full sunlight and only moderate watering at any time.

C. sulcolanata is a clustering species, having tubercles 5-angled at the base. Spines brownish with black tips. Flowers very large, pinkish.

C. clava is bluish green in colour with openly disposed tubercles bearing yellowish or brown spines. Tends to become cylindrical. Large flowers mainly yellow with greenish and reddish markings.

C. palmeri has yellow flowers with brownish stripes on the outer surface. Areoles on young plants are very woolly.

Discocactus (South America)

A remarkable genus which has had several new species discovered in recent years. The plant body is globose and somewhat flattened. With maturity a cephalium forms, from which the flowers protrude. All species are rather difficult in cultivation and require a higher temperature than most other genera.

D. alteolens is a very flattish plant with only few ribs and spines and large white flowers.

D. heptacanthus, native of Brazil has about 12 tuberculate ribs and distinctive recurved radial spines. Flowers are large, white and fragrant. *D. horstii* found in south Brazil a few years ago has proved the smallest species of the genus so far discovered. It has about 20 acute ribs, closely set areoles and minute comb-like spines. Large white flowers emerge from the small woolly cephalium, often larger than the plant body.

Disocactus (Central America)

A fascinating genus of epiphytic cacti—all with strap-like leaves and flowers varying from whitish to scarlet. Most species flower during the English winter months, so care must be taken to maintain sufficient warmth.

D. biformis has long branches, fleshy and serrated. Flower is long and slender, magenta, with purple style. Native of Guatemala and Honduras.

D. macranthus (*Pseudorhipsalis macrantha*). A very easy flowering plant with elongated stems and crenated edges. The fragrant yellowish cream flowers appear early in the year. Native of Chiapas, Mexico.

D. nelsonii (*Chiapasia nelsonii*) and its variety *hondurensis* have long purplish pink trumpet flowers, but are short-lived. Stem growth is pendent with many flattened branches. Requires really warm conditions.

Echinocactus (Mexico)

Large growing barrel-shaped plants, very many spines and usually only small flowers. Commonly called the hedgehog cactus which exemplifies the plant—the Greek *echinos* means 'hedgehog'.

Fig. 7.
Echinocactus
grusonii.

25

E. grusonii is one of the most spectacular cacti in cultivation—from young plants to full maturity they cannot be surpassed with their golden-yellow spines and remarkable growth. Called the Golden Barrel—it is well named—and has quite small bright yellow flowers in maturity (Fig. 7).

Echinocereus (Mexico and western U.S.A.)

Plants with normally large colourful, long-lasting flowers. The majority are very spiny and low-growing, frequently forming large clumps. Not difficult in cultivation, but they prefer to be kept completely dry during the winter months. Only a few of this large genus can be mentioned, but all are worthy of note.

E. blanckii is a low growing, semi-erect plant with prominently tuberculate ribs and brown or blackish spines. Flowers are large, about 3 in. (7 cm) diameter, purplish red.

E. reichenbachii has close-set pectinate spines and attractive pink and white flowers.

E. engelmannii is rather variable in spination, sometimes with blackish tips, others with brown or yellow. Stems grow to about 8 in. (20 cm) tall and form largish clumps. Flowers purple-red.

E. pulchellus is globular in shape, bluish green in colour with about 12 ribs and small areoles bearing 3–4 very short yellow spines. Flowers are white to deep rose.

E. knippelianus, another distinctive species of smaller growth. Globular in shape with five prominent ribs, woolly areoles and few thin spines. Free flowering in spring, vivid pale magenta flowers.

E. viridiflorus has small globular plants with variegated white and reddish spines, and a greenish flower.

Echinofossulocactus (Mexico)

Globular plants with thin, wavy, deeply grooved ribs. Spines are usually long and somewhat flattened, often forming a mass of entangled spines at the crown. These are sun loving plants, requiring a well drained soil and frequent watering during the growing season. Also referred to as *Stenocactus*.

E. coptonogonus has only about 14 deeply notched ribs with areoles well apart and soft incurved flattened spines, reddish when young. Flowers are mauve or pinkish purple.

E. multicostatus has over 100 narrow ribs, few areoles and elongated, flexible erect, spreading spines. Flowers are large, pinkish white.

E. violaciflorus has somewhat fewer wavy ribs and very attractive whitish flowers veined purple.

Echinopsis (South America) (see also *Trichocereus* and *Helianthocereus*).

This genus has been considerably increased numerically due to the merging of *Trichocereus* with it. This might well prove a group for further research. The original species of the genus are well-known and easily grown plants—flowering freely in cultivation, although only short lived, lasting but a day.

E. eyriesii is a globular plant, native of South Brazil and Argentina, with many acute ribs and short spines. Large fragrant white flowers are produced from the side of the plant.

E. multiplex is very similar in many respects to the above, but has longer spines. It offsets freely and has large pink flowers.

E. leucantha is an oblong shaped plant with about 15 ribs, curved brownish spines and one long central curved spine. Flowers are very large,white and scented.

Fig. 8. A group of Echinopsis and Trichocereus species.

Epiphyllum (Mexico, West Indies and South America)
All species are epiphytic having long flattened stems, sometimes crenated with areoles along the margins and spineless in maturity. All are of fairly easy culture, requiring an acid soil and a temperature of 12°C (55°F) for good results. All flowers are white, creamy white or faintly yellow. Some species are used for pollinating with plants of other genera to produce the exotic 'orchid' cacti cultivars.

E. anguliger has deeply toothed margins along the flat branches and fragrant white flowers which bloom by day.

E. crenatum is a species used more for hybridising than any other. Has thick glaucous branches and large scented white flowers, opening by day and long lasting.

27

E. caudatum has elongated lanceolate stems and branches, with undulating margins and no spines. A Mexican species with white scented flowers, night flowering.

E. chrysocardium (Heart of Gold) is a more recent discovery and the largest species of the genus. Has very wide stems, very deeply crenated with huge pure white flowers and pronounced golden filaments—hence its name.

Espostoa (Peru and Equador)

Most attractive nocturnal flowering cacti of columnar habit, often with long whitish hairs where pseudocephalium develops with maturity. Requires full sun, watering in moderation. All known members of the genus are easy to grow.

E. lanata from an altitude of over 2000 m. White hairs with yellow to red spines makes this a most interesting plant. Flowers rather small, developing through the cephalium.

E. melanostele is a more robust species with brownish cephalium and pinkish white flowers.

Ferocactus (Mexico, south-west U.S.A.)

Large barrel-shaped plants with strong spines, these being straight, curved, hooked or a combination thereof. The spines are a main feature, quickly producing their true form as quite young plants. A porous soil is essential, a sunny position and plenty of water during the growing season. Of easy culture, but not quick growing.

F. acanthodes has distinctive red and bright yellow spines, densely arranged. It flowers from near the crown of plant, yellow or pale orange. Easy to grow from seed.

F. viridescens is a smaller growing species from south California and Baja. New spines are red, gradually fading to pink. Flowers greenish yellow and rather small.

F. fordii is also of smaller growth and grows in Baja, California. Flowers are pinkish rose and form in a ring around the crown.

Frailea (Brazil and Paraguay)

All species are of relatively small growth, almost miniatures. Mostly globular, occasionally becoming elongated and grouping. Flowers are pollinated without actually opening.

F. cataphracta, native of Paraguay. Small growing to only about an inch (2 cm) diameter. Dull purplish green in colour with low ribs, flattened tubercles and minute spines. Yellow flowers open in full sunshine.

F. matoana, a recent discovery in south Brazil, has a reddish brown body, globular tubercles and very small spines. Flowers are brown and yellow.

Gymnocalycium (South America)

A very popular genus with chin-shaped tubercles. Plant surface usually smooth and waxy. Flowers are usually bell-shaped. Of easy culture, requiring partial shade during the height of summer, and ample watering in warmest weather.

G. mihanovitchii has a greyish green body with reddish markings forming transverse bands around the plant. Flowers are yellow, or yellowish white. There are varieties of the species, of which *friedrichiae* has rose-pink flowers. Seedlings of these often germinate pink or yellow—and these are used for grafting to produce the red or yellow 'knobs' commercially available. Argentina.

G. horstii has a dark green glossy body and few well defined ribs, felted areoles with radial spines and often a long central one. Flowers are peach-pink and long lasting. Brazil.

G. saglione, one of the larger species, even to 14 in. (28 cm) high. Chins are very pronounced, these having brownish red or greyish curved spines. Flowers pinkish white. Argentina.

Fig. 9. Gymnocalycium saglione.

Haageocereus (South America)

A most variable genus, some with erect or semi-erect growth, others sprawling and clambering. Nearly all species are associated with golden-yellow spines with just a few exceptions.

H. versicolor is a species from Peru of slender erect growth with many ribs and densely covered with reddish brown and yellow spines. Flowers are white.

29

H. decumbens from the borders of Peru and Chile is of clambering habit, with many low ribs completely hidden by masses of golden yellow spines. Flowers white.

Harrisia (West Indies)

A genus closely related to *Eriocereus* of South American habitats— species of both genera are often confused. Plants of vigorous growth and easy culture.

H. gracilis, a native of Jamaica, is tall growing and much branched with up to 11 ribs. Spines are white, tipped black. Flowers white, very large with long brownish green tube. Perhaps this is better known under the name, *H. repandus*.

Hatiora (Brazil)

Spineless epiphytic plants consisting of many very small cylindrical joints. Branches can be many and have either an erect or semi pendent habit. Related to *Rhipsalis*.

H. salicornioides is a low bushy plant with small joints that are almost bottle shaped. Terminal joints have woolly areoles. Flowers orange yellow from the terminals.

H. bambusoides is very similar but with more cylindrical segments. Flowers orange.

Helianthocereus (Bolivia, Argentina)

Generally of clustering habit forming clumps of many semi-erect or prostrate stems. Closely related to *Trichocereus* and *Lobivia* and now united with *Echinopsis*. Of easy culture, requiring a sunny position.

H. huasha. A low growing plant of many semi-erect cylindrical stems each with about 18 low rounded ribs, having closely set areoles with numerous yellowish brown spines. Flowers are either red or yellow.

H. grandiflorus is a smaller growing plant with more stunted growth, clustering freely. Stems have many yellowish radial spines. Flowers pink.

Heliocereus (Mexico, Guatemala)

Clambering or semi erect plants with 3–4 angled stems, areoles set well apart, large and felted with stiffish spines. Flowers exceedingly beautiful —some species used for cross pollinating with *Epiphyllum* to produce 'orchid' cacti cultivars.

H. speciosus is a popular species from central and southern Mexico, having large rich scarlet flowers. Generally of semi-erect habit, stems 3–4 angled and yellow spines. Used for hybridising with *Epiphyllum*. Var. *superbus* has even larger flowers flushed lilac-purple. Var. *amecamensis* is of more prostrate habit with white flowers.

Hylocereus (Mexico, Venezuela, Peru, West Indies)

All are climbing vine-like plants with differing stem formations, but usually 3-angled. All are considered epiphytic and are associated with forest conditions in habitat. Most species are of easy culture, requiring an acid compost and regular watering during summer months. Nocturnal flowering.

H. undatus is the most common of this genus with definite 3-angled stems and climbing to many metres in length. Flowers are large, nocturnal, sweetly scented and creamy white in colour.

H. calcaratus from Costa Rica and possibly northwards through Guatemala to southern Mexico. Stems very fresh-green and prominent marginal lobes and scarcely spined. Flowers are large creamy-white with bright orange-yellow stamens. A temperature of 12°C (55°F) is needed.

H. purpusii is from western Mexico and very similar to *H. undatus* in stem form, but often bluish green and horny-margined. Flowers large, white to golden-yellow.

Lemaireocereus (Mexico and central America)

Tall growing columnar plants, often forming thick clumps. All are well-known in cultivation and respond readily to greenhouse conditions. Require a sunny position and good watering during warmest months.

L. thurberi has wide distribution in Arizona, northern Mexico and Baja. A stout, much branched plant forming clumps that grow to many metres high in habitat. Stems are dark brownish green with low ribs and large brown felted areoles, spines numerous. Flowers large, whitish.

Lepismium (South America)

Epiphytic plants related to *Rhipsalis*. All species have a sunken ovary, thus distinguishing them from *Rhipsalis*. All require an acid compost and humid conditions.

L. cruciforme is found growing on rocks in forest areas. Generally with triangular stems, elongated, purplish green or reddish in colour. Flowers white and fruits reddish purple. Var. *myosurus* has more slender stems of same colouring with pink flowers.

L. paradoxum is better known as *Rhipsalis paradoxa*. A unique species with link-like stem growth, developing in whorls. Flowers and fruits are white. Native of Brazil.

Leuchtenbergia (Mexico)

A monotypic genus containing an extraordinary plant looking very much like an *Agave*. Requires a loose, fairly rich soil and moderate watering only in the growing season.

L. principis has a fairly small cylindrical body but long 3-angled finger-like tubercles, often to 5 in. (12 cm) long. These have paper-like spines at the tips. Flowers are large and yellow, very fragrant and long lasting.

Lobivia (South America) see also *Chamaecereus*

A genus of low growing, globose plants, many species of which offset freely. All have very colourful, decorative flowers which bloom in daytime. A rather rich soil is preferable, with free watering in warmer weather. They are closely related to *Echinopsis* and *Rebutia*.

L. ferox is quite a large Bolivian species with many very long upcurved spines, some of which can be 6 in. (15 cm) long. Flowers reddish.

31

L. hertrichiana is a smaller growing species, in habitat mainly solitary, but in cultivation clusters freely. The body is glossy green with brownish spines and bright scarlet flowers.

L. leptacantha, a newly discovered Peruvian plant found at 3000 m. altitude. The stems are bright green with long yellowish brown spines, the flowers somewhat variable in colour—reddish orange or yellowish orange—large and long lasting.

Lophophora (Texas, Mexico)

Spineless globular plants, dull bluish green body with a few rather obscure ribs; and areoles with tufts of hairs. Commonly called the peyote, the juice extracted from the plants is said to cause hallucinations. Use loose, sandy soil, preferably with a little lime added, and give full sun and moderate watering in warmest weather.

L. williamsii and the other species comprising the genus, *L. lutea* and *L. diffusa* together with several different varieties of the type species, are very similar in most respects—all are of easy culture, a number are rare, and flower colours vary from white to deep pink.

Machaeorcereus (Mexico)

A small genus of two species. Both have long branches with many vicious spines. They are not often seen in cultivation, possibly on account of their large growth. However, they are not too demanding in their requirements; an open soil, full sun and regular watering throughout the growing season will give good results.

M. eruca (Creeping Devil) is one of the most spectacular cacti, growing to 15 m. or more in length. The stems are closely set with large spines. Flowers are red, small, bell-shaped and appear towards the tips of the stems. *M. gummosus* is less barbed and is of more erect growth.

Mammillaria (Mexico, U.S.A. and West Indies)

One of the largest genera containing over 200 species—mainly small growing, invariably offsetting freely—a few remain solitary. Flowers are small, but freely produced over a period of many weeks. A rich porous soil is necessary for these to thrive, together with full sun and adequate watering in growing season. Should be kept completely dry in winter.

M. candida is an attractive globular species, rarely offsetting, with numerous white spines completely covering the body. A beautiful species with pink flowers.

M. elongata is one of the best known of this genus—somewhat cylindrical stems that develop upright clusters. Spines variable, white, yellow, brown or darker. Flowers are not prolific but fairly constant throughout the flowering season—they can vary from white to yellowish.

M. plumosa: a much sought after clustering species completely covered with white feathery spines. Flowers white, flushed pink. Requires a rich limy soil, this enabling the plant to maintain its whiteness.

M. goldii represents the more miniature species. Of fairly recent introduc-

Fig. 10. Mammillaria elongata.

tion, found at over 1000 m. altitude in Sonora. Stems are usually simple, rarely offsetting, sub-globose with small tubercles in spirals. Areoles with numerous pectinate, minute spines which interlace. Flower lilac-pink and larger than the plant.

M. hahniana, a charming white spined and hairy species (see front cover) from Mexico at an altitude of nearly 2000 m. The red flowers appear in a circle around the crown of the plant.

M. spinosissima—a fine species usually of solitary growth to about 10 in. (25 cm) tall. Spine colouring most variable, ranging from yellowish white to brownish red. Flowers carmine-red.

M. zeilmanniana can be either solitary or may grow in tufts. Body dark green with many whitish hair-like radial spines and hooked red-tipped brownish centrals. Flowers are numerous and long lasting, reddish purple. Very suitable for either home or greenhouse, giving full sun for best results and free watering in growing season, dry thereafter.

Mediocactus (South America, Martinique)
A small genus of semi-erect, free branching clambering plants, all are epiphytes. Still quite uncommon in cultivation although they are by no means difficult to grow. All species are night flowering. Rich acid soil is essential, but this must be porous. Minimum temperature 12°C (55°F).

M. coccineus is native of Brazil and has dark green 3-angled stems with beak-like projections just below the areoles and very small spines. Aerial roots occur on the stems and aid its climbing habit. Flowers are very large, pure white and scented. The specific title refers to the fruit which is bright red in colour.

M. megalanthus is a very rare plant from Peru and Bolivia and has masses of pendent stems with undulating margins and brownish spines. The flowers are scented, large, and pure white in colour—considered one of the largest cactus flowers, frequently to 15 in. (38 cm) long.

Melocactus (Mexico, West Indies, South America)

A fascinating genus commonly known as turks' cap cactus, due to the development of a distinctive cephalium from the crown of the plant. Most species are considered difficult and no doubt require a little more attention than most. All appreciate a high temperature throughout the year, 18°–20°C (64°–68°F) is advisable. A rich soil with ample humus helps the healthy development of the plants. Flowers emerge through the cephalium.

M. broadwayii from the West Indies, has a broad base gradually narrowing towards the cephalium, about 18 ribs with regularly set areoles and yellowish brown spines. Cephalium consists of dense soft brown hairs and white wool. Flower purplish red.

M. glaucescens has a greyish blue body, about 11 broad ribs, well set areoles and greyish spines. This red flowering species is one of the more recent discoveries from south Brazil.

Mila (Peru)

All species are of caespitose habit with rather small flowers. The generic name is an anagram of the Peruvian capital, Lima; not frequently seen in cultivation. A warm sunny position in the greenhouse is recommended, with a lime-free and very porous soil.

M. caespitosa, a small plant growing to about 6 in. (15 cm) high and clumping freely. Areoles are densely brown-felted with many yellowish brown spines. Flowers yellow, borne at apex of stems.

Monvillea (South America)

All species are of erect or semi-erect growth with slender stems, night flowering on a long tube. The flower is unusual in having the stamens scattered over the throat instead of being in definite rows. All are of easy culture in a good light position, open rich soil and with moderate watering.

M. cavendishii originates from Brazil, Paraguay and northern Argentina. Tall growing, branching from the base. Stems with few rounded ribs and about 12 brown spines to each areole. Flowers white, about 5 in. (12 cm) long.

M. spegazzini has most attractive bluish green stems, marbled white and grey, generally 3-angled with large tubercles and black-spined areoles. Flowers whitish pink.

Myrtillocactus (Mexico, Guatemala)

In nature, plants have a tree-like growth, branching freely. Flowers are rather small, fruits of certain species are edible and when dried resemble raisins. Prefers a soil with lime included and very open. Moderate watering and only during growing season.

M. geometrizens from central Mexico has unusually bluish green stems, few ribs and areoles set well apart bearing blackish spines. Flowers creamy-yellow, fruits bluish. Young plants make excellent grafting stock.

Neolloydia (Mexico, Texas)

A small genus of cylindrical plants, tubercles similar to *Mammillaria*, and many spines. Culture should be a little more precise than with some genera, porous soil, full sun but more restrictive with water. Minimum temperature of 8°C (46°F) is advisable, and then the plants should be completely dry.

N. grandiflora. An outstanding species having large reddish purple flowers. Stem solitary, brownish green; many radial and few central spines, yellowish brown and blackish. Flowers from crown of plant.

N. texensis has small clustering stems, many white spreading radial spines and long black central spines. This and the preceding are now considered varieties of *N. conoidea*.

Neoporteria (Chile and Peru)

A large genus which has been the subject of considerable re-classification in recent years. Plants with globular or cylindrical shaped stems, usually with many ribs and many or few spines. Culture requires an acid, open compost, a higher temperature than many other genera as many species flower late or very early in the year.

N. subgibbosa becomes more elongated with maturity. The body is pale green with about 20 ribs, many protruding chin-like tubercles and areoles bearing many sharp, erect, yellowish brown spines. Flowers are pinkish red on a yellowish tube. Native of Chile.

N. fusca (*Neochilenia fusca*), globular, becoming cylindrical, about 3½ in. (9 cm) diameter. Usually about 12 ribs with protruding tubercles, white woolly areoles and about 8 black spines turning greyish. Flowers greenish yellow. Of Chilean origin.

N. villosa has attractive greyish green stems, slightly tinged with purple, and spirally arranged ribs, about 15 in number; closely set white woolly areoles, yellow spines and long bristly hairs standing erect. Flowers are white, tipped pink, tubes with reddish scales.

Nopalxochia (Mexico)

A small family of true epiphytes, having *Epiphyllum*-like foliage, but smaller flowers. Excellent plants for home culture, mostly with semipendent habit, flowers produced freely and long lasting. A rich acid and porous soil is essential; a light, but shaded, position; and moderate watering throughout the year.

N. phyllanthoides is the best-known species. Thin, flattened stems having crenated margins bearing many charming, long-lasting, pinkish flowers in early spring. The cultivar, 'Deutsche Kaiserin' is perhaps even better known due to the more robust growth and slightly larger flowers.

Notocactus (South America)

Another of the most popular genera of Cactaceae—all globular or semi-columnar in shape, most variable in spination, and generally very free flowering. A loose rich soil should be used, not too full sun, and regular watering throughout the growing season. Useful for home or greenhouse.

N. ottonis has a wide distribution in south Brazil, Uruguay, Argentina and Paraguay. Species from different areas have varying characteristics in both spine formation and flower colour. Plants to about 4 in. (10 cm) diameter, about 12 ribs, areoles with yellowish and brownish red spines. Flowers golden-yellow, shiny, reddish stigma and lobes; flower tube covered with brown hairs.

N. leninghausii is a beautiful species with columnar stem, somewhat flattened on top or slightly slanted. Spines are numerous, golden-yellow, hair-like, from closely set areoles. Large golden-yellow flowers appear in the crown of the plant and remain for many days.

N. scopa is cylindrical in form, widening towards the top. Spines are generally white with an intermingling of brownish or reddish tipped spines. The flowers borne in a circle around the crown are rich canary-yellow with a red stigma. Native of south Brazil and Uruguay.

Fig. 11. Various species of Notocactus.

36

Nyctocereus (Mexico and central America)

Erect growing plants, becoming semi-prostrate, slender stems with flowers arising from near the tips of the shoots, usually pointing upwards. Robust plants preferring a high temperature during the growing season with free watering, but kept dry and cool in winter.

N. serpentinus is a typical snake cactus, as its specific names suggests. Erect at first, then becoming prostrate and creeping. Has about 12 flat rounded ribs, woolly areoles and whitish,brown-tipped spines. Flowers are nocturnal, strongly scented, white flushed green or brown.

N. chontalensis is an uncommon species with more angular-shaped stems, semi-erect growth and whitish night-flowering blooms.

Opuntia (southern Canada to southern Argentina)

A vast genus which now embraces several obsolete genera—*Corynopuntia, Cylindropuntia, Austrocylindropuntia* and others—these having, in some instances, become sub-genera. In general they are all of easy culture, although there are exceptions. An open soil is essential with full sun and plenty of water in growing season, but completely dry in resting period. Many species have to attain a good age before flowering, this seems particularly to apply to those with cylindrical stems. The fruits are referred to as prickly pears.

O. basilaris has obovate blue-green or purplish pads and many areoles with glochids but no spines. Flowers are pinkish purple. Variety *cordata* has heart-shaped pads.

O. gosseliniana is an attractive species with almost circular pads becoming bluish grey when mature. Long bristle-like spines to about 3 in. (8 cm) long and bright yellow flowers make this a very desirable plant. Variety *santa-rita* has similar characteristics, but the pads are even more blue and tinged purple, with very long black spines at the top of the pads. Flowers are deep yellow with orange-red throat. According to American botanists, both of these are now considered varieties of *O. violacea*.

O. curassivica is a low growing species from the more southerly islands of the West Indies. Joints are small, narrow and somewhat flattened with areoles bearing yellow spines and woolly hairs. Flowers yellow.

O. microdasys is probably the best known of the family, a typical rabbit ears plant which is variable in spine coloration. The oval pads have a polka-dot effect, being closely but regularly covered by areoles with sharp bristly glochids—areoles can be yellow, white (var. *alba*) or brownish red (var. *rufida*). Native of north Mexico.

O. subulata has long cylindrical stems with no ribs. Fleshy leaves develop on new growth, but these rapidly fall off, although occasionally in cultivation are found to be rather persistent. A Peruvian species with yellow or orange-yellow flowers.

Oreocereus (Bolivia, Chile, Peru)

A small group of cereoid cacti, very ornamental and of fairly easy culture.

All species have large areoles, many spines and long hairs. A good sunny position is advised, fairly open rich soil and regular watering and feeding during the growing season. They tolerate low temperatures so long as the soil is completely dry. Suitable for home or greenhouse.

O. celsianus and its several varieties are all spectacular plants, varying principally in spine and hair colouring. *O. celsianus* itself has yellow spines, brownish whitish hairs and red flowers. Var. *trollii* is outstanding with yellow spines, long pure white hairs and wool. Flowers rich carmine-red, sometimes rose-pink. Var. *ritteri* is of more slender growth with yellowish brown spines and hairs, flowers orange-red.

Oroya (Peru)

A small but handsome genus of few species and several varieties, all semi-globose in shape with elongated areoles and widely spreading spines. They are native of high altitudes at nearly 4000 m., requiring a really warm position is summer and cool in winter. A rich compost is recommended with regular feeding in warm weather. Sometimes considered difficult to flower—but they enjoy good sunlight and a nutritious, open soil, and given this they will flower quite readily.

O. peruviana has a somewhat depressed body, deep green in colour, broad ribs and protruding tubercles. Areoles with whitish wool and about 20 brown spines and a few slender white hairs. Flowers develop in rings around the crown, nearly an inch (2·5 cm) long, bright orange-red.

O. borchersii is a more cylindrical-shaped plant but still tending to be rather globular. Light green in colour with broader areoles, brownish yellow spines and greenish yellow flowers.

Pachycereus (Mexico)

A small genus of very large growing plants—including some of the largest of the Cactaceae. Generally tree-like in their growth, having a shorter trunk and many ascending branches. Young plants make attractive specimens for home or greenhouse, but require the brightest position possible with plenty of water in growing season. They take many years to reach an 'uncontrollable' height.

P. pringlei is the best known and deservedly popular in the genus. In habitat this may reach eventually 12 m. tall. Robust and spiney with about 15 obtuse ribs, large brown-felted areoles with densely black-tipped spines, it is worthy of inclusion in any collection. Flowers are produced on mature plants, whitish, about 8 cm long, the tube being covered with small scales and brownish hairs.

Parodia (South America)

Many species are included in this very interesting genus—all have rather small, globose bodies, solitary and generally most floriferous. They are good houseplants, requiring a reasonably bright position, regular watering and feeding in warm weather, and, if temperatures justify, not completely dry in winter. If temperatures are low, then dry off completely. Soil should be porous, rich with humus for best results—often the more open the soil, the better the results.

P. chrysacanthion is exceedingly beautiful, having about 20 ribs divided into tubercles, each areole having numerous bright golden-yellow spines, almost completely covering the plant body. The crown is even more densely spined from whence woolly flower buds develop and emerge, opening deep yellow. They flower as quite young plants. Native of northern Argentina.

P. brevihamata is a much smaller species, having an olive-green body with about 22 ribs, tubercles being spirally arranged; white woolly areoles with many yellowish white spines, the centrals having brownish tips, one of which points downwards and is hooked. Flowers are quite large, rich golden-yellow. Endemic to Brazil.

P. sanguiniflora, a Bolivian species, is rightly named on account of its deep-red flower. The body is fresh green, globose, tubercles cone-shaped and arranged spirally, areoles numerous, but the centrals are reddish brown and hooked at the tip.

P. microsperma grows to about 4 in. (10 cm) diameter, areoles have whitish radial spines and 3–4 reddish brown centrals, the lowest one being hooked at the tip. Flowers bright yellow. The specific name means small seeds— and this is actually a characteristic of all *Parodia* species.

Fig. 12.
Parodia
chrysocanthion.

39

Pereskia (Mexico, Bolivia, Peru)

Vine-like plants, sometimes developing treelike proportions, but invariably of clambering habit. Stems are long, slender and bear true leaves, generally very spiney, and, if given correct conditions, very free-flowering. Principally for greenhouse decoration. An open soil is necessary and preferably temperatures not less than 10°C (50°F). Water well during the summer. *P. aculeata* is native to more tropical regions and needs warmth at all times. A very free-branching species with elliptical dark-green leaves and scented, creamy-yellow flowers produced in clusters. Sections of young growth, taken as cuttings and rooted, are often used as grafting stock for smaller growing cacti and *Schlumbergera*.

P. grandifolia was for long known as *Rhodocactus grandifolius*. A treelike plant with large oblong-shaped leaves, rather spiney, and very attractive lilac-rose flowers from the terminals of the stems. A native of West Indies.

Pilosocereus (Mexico, West Indies, South America)

A large genus of tall growing plants, mostly developing pseudocephaliums with maturity. The majority of species prefer a reasonably warm condition, ample watering during the growing season. Soil must be very porous and rich in humus. Primarily for greenhouse culture.

P. palmeri (*Cephalocereus palmeri*) has stout bluish green columnar habit with about 8–9 prominent ribs with regularly set white woolly areoles, each with about 10 radial spines and a long central spine. The apex becomes densely covered with masses of white wool after a few years through which appear reddish white flowers, about 2 in. (5 cm) diameter, lasting for several days. Native of eastern Mexico.

P. glaucescens is of Brazilian origin—tall, erect, bluish green stems, rounded ribs, close set areoles with many white bristles and hairs, spines yellowish brown. This is now better referred to as *Pseudopilosocereus glaucescens*.

Pterocactus (Argentina)

A small genus included under the prickly pear group, having the unusual characteristic of forming a large tuberous root system. Another feature is the winged seeds peculiar only to this genus within the Cactaceae. Not difficult in cultivation so long as ample room is given for the roots—otherwise it might be wise to graft on to species of *Opuntia*.

P. tuberosus has brownish green stems, cylindrical, and covered with numerous, minute, whitish hairy spines. Flowers are bright yellow, about an inch (2·5 cm) diameter.

Rebutia (South America)

A popular genus comprising many species, small globular plants, rarely short cylindrical and usually freely clustering. They have no distinctive ribs, but many small tubercles fairly regularly arranged. Cultivation and propagation are easy. Soil should be rich and porous, half-shade will help to avoid dehydration. Regular watering throughout the growing season and suitable fertilizing periodically will ensure good flowering plants. All make excellent home or greenhouse plants.

R. marsoneri from N. Argentina has dark green body, many yellowish brown spines and pale to deep yellow flowers. *R. senilis* var. *kesselringiana* is another yellow flowering species, although the globular body has many longish white hairs and spines.

R. minuscula, a very free-clustering species from N. Argentina, is undoubtedly the best known of the genus, having a glossy green body, many short whitish spines, and bright red flowers which appear on very young plants.

R. fiebrigii, a short cylindrical, glossy-green plant has numerous bristly white spines and bright orange-red flowers. Native of Bolivia.

Many differing colorations of flowers are represented within the genus— white, in the case of *R. albiflora*; pink with *R. minuscula* var. *kariusiana* and purple in *R. minuscula* var. *violaciflora*.

Rhipsalidopsis (Brazil)

A small genus of epiphytic cacti, having small flattish segments, these being sometimes 3–5 angled. Rich, acid compost is essential with moisture available throughout the year, although in moderation during the rest period. Ideal for house or greenhouse cultivation.

R. gaertneri is the Easter cactus, having bright green stems with occasional purplish markings on the margins. Flowers from the tip of the segments, bright red to scarlet.

R. rosea, a very well-known popular species of somewhat shrubby habit but inclined to be pendent. Flowers are rose-pink, appearing in late spring. From south Brazil.

Rhipsalis (South America, West Indies, Madagascar)

One of the most 'un-understandable' genera of the whole family—it comprises so many differing forms and peculiarities, together with changeable characteristics within a species, that some are still in doubt as to their correct nomenclature. All are epiphytic or saxicolous, the majority are without spines, whilst flowers are usually small but regular in shape. Fruits are small berries with very small seeds. Of easy culture, using acid compost, half-light position, and no drying-out. Suitable for hanging basket culture.

R. capilliformis is representative of the long pendent species with almost thread-like stems to 24 in. (60 cm) or more in length. Flowers are white and numerous. S. Brazil.

R. houlletiana. One of the best known species with flat, leaf-like stems, pale fresh green in colour and pronounced crenations. Flowers bell-shaped, creamy-white. S. Brazil.

R. teres also has cylindrical stems, somewhat stouter and much-branched, with pinkish areoles and semi-erect growth. An eastern Brazil species with creamy-yellow flowers.

R. tonduzii has 3 to 5-angled stems and branches, becoming elongated and semi-bushy. Areoles are closely set, small white flowers and white fruits. Native of Costa Rica.

R. warmingiana has long strap-like stems, rarely 3-angled with crenate margins. Flowers are quite large, white—bell-shaped. Fruits are first red turning black. Brazil.

Schlumbergera

This small genus includes many familiar houseplants, particularly those autumn and winter-flowering types known as *Zygocactus*. This latter group of plants is mainly of epiphytic origin, and are very popular in cultivation. Stems are flattened, divided into short segments with pronounced teeth on upper part. Flowers are zygomorphic and these develop at the apex of the segments.

S. truncata has dark green segments with very apparent teeth. Flowers magenta with white filaments and purple style. A parent of the generally recognised Christmas cactus with rounded segments. There are varieties and cultivars of the species; 'Delicatus' has pure white flowers with rich magenta style, and a seedling of 'Delicatus'—'Pink Beauty'—gained a First Class Certificate in the Schlumbergera Trials held at Wisley in 1975/7. 'Wintermärchen' also has white flowers, flushed pink and is more sturdy than 'Delicatus'. Other fascinating cultivars include 'Frankenstolz' with rose-pink petal and white throat; 'Weihnachtsfreude', pale orange-tinged magenta; 'Lilofee', pale magenta with lighter central stripe; 'Noris', which has deep rich magenta and red-orange flowers. These and others are all of easy culture so long as they are kept warm during the flowering season—a temperature of 15°C (59°F) is essential if plants are to flourish. Regular feeding from the time when the buds form and throughout the growing period is recommended—and always a rich acid, porous compost, which is never allowed to dry out completely.

Selenicereus (Mexico, Central and Southern America, West Indies)

An interesting genus of climbing, clambering plants, most of which can be classified as epiphytic. Most species are adaptable for greenhouse culture, requiring a good root area and ample space to trail. Acid soil is best, but this should be porous. Flowers nocturnal.

S. grandiflorus, commonly called Queen of the Night, is from Jamaica, Cuba and other West Indian islands. Stems dark green, with 5–8 ribs having small brownish spines. Flowers very large and scented, often to 8 in. (22 cm) long. Rooted cuttings of suitable length make excellent grafting stock.

S. pringlei is a more uncommon species. Stems are quite thick with 6–7 ribs, numerous yellowish spines and whitish bristles which densely cover the stems. Flowers creamy-yellow, about 7 in. (18 cm) diameter.

S. wercklei is a definite epiphyte, in appearance very similar to *Rhipsalis*. Flowers are large, white, about 6 in. (15 cm) diameter. Endemic to Costa Rica.

Soehrensia (Argentina, Chile)

A small but important genus closely allied to *Lobivia* and *Echinopsis*. Fairly large globular plants with rather small funnel-shaped flowers on a short tube, which is hairy, but without bristles. Of easy culture, requiring rich open soil, full sun, moderate watering in summer, completely dry in winter. For greenhouse culture.

S. bruchii. An impressive species with greyish green body, about 50 ribs, areoles with whitish wool and spreading, protruding spines. Flowers develop near the crown, deep red.

Fig. 13. Soehrensia bruchii.

Stetsonia (Argentina)

An attractive genus embracing only one species *S. coryne*—a tree-like plant of stout growth and spectacular spination. A well known plant in cultivation requiring a well-drained porous soil, rich in humus, a sunny position and moderate watering in the growing season, otherwise kept dry. Minimum temperature about 10°C (50°F).

43

S. coryne has pale green stems with 7–9 obtuse ribs, woolly areoles with about 10 strong greyish black spines of unequal length. Flowers are nocturnal and only develop on very mature plants—these are white, about 6 in. (15 cm) long and appear from the sides of the plant.

Fig. 14.
Stetsonia coryne.

Sulcorebutia (Bolivia)
An intriguing genus of grouping species, usually with very pronounced areoles and most colourful flowers. Very suitable for greenhouse culture, although still considered by some to require grafting for best results. This method of culture is undoubtedly helpful, but with few exceptions they thrive on their own roots if a rich compost is provided and the temperature does not fall under 10°C (50°F) in winter.
S. steinbachii was the original species discovered and is still very popular. A small globular plant which clusters freely, dark-green body, tuberculate ribs and long narrow areoles with small spreading brown spines. Flowers are deep blood-red.

S. glomeriseta has a stem densely covered with numerous small white bristle-like spines; the flowers are bright yellow.

S. menesesii has pinkish white pectinate spines, somewhat bristle-like, also with yellow flowers.

Tacinga (Brazil)

Another genus of the prickly pear group for long recognised as a mono-typic genus, but new research has included another species and variety. Tall growing plants of easy culture, requiring similar attention to species of *Opuntia*.

T. funalis has erect cylindrical greyish blue branches with scarcely discernible ribs, having areoles with rather deciduous glochids and occasional soft brownish spines. Flowers are greenish white from the tips of the branches. *T. atropurpurea* and its variety *zehntnerioides* have similar characteristics.

Tephrocactus (South America)

According to certain authorities this genus has now been merged with *Opuntia*, but because of particular features they are here recorded separately. All are of low growing habit, forming clumps or clusters. Stem growth varies with the species, some being globular, others sub-cylindrical. A fascinating sub-genus, most species being of reasonably easy culture given a rich porous soil, excellent drainage, good light position and a temperature of at least 10°C (50°F) recommended for safety.

T. lagapus (or *Opuntia lagopus*) is possibly a synonym of *T. floccosa*. These have somewhat oblong joints with whitish or yellowish white long hairs almost covering the joints completely. Flowers yellow.

T. ignescens (or *Opuntia ignescens*) is an interesting Peruvian species with bluish green spreading joints, forming clusters, few areoles with yellow spines. Flowers scarlet.

T. molinensis (or *Opuntia molinensis*). A spineless plant of small elliptic segments, dark greyish green with densely brown-tufted areoles. Considered difficult on its own roots, so best grafted on to *Opuntia*. A very distinctive species from Argentina.

T. ovatus (or *Opuntia ovata*) is a compact dwarf plant which forms quite dense clumps. Segments are yellowish green, spines of unequal length usually on the upper part of the segments—brownish yellow in colour. Flower pale golden-yellow. Native of Argentina and Chile.

Thelocactus (Mexico, U.S.A.)

A very colourful genus of globular plants, all of which are of easy culture. They are all sun-lovers, requiring a moderately rich, porous compost— and are best suited for greenhouse cultivation.

T. bicolor has a wide distribution from southern Texas to central Mexico. Ribs are few, these being somewhat spirally arranged with long tubercles. Spines are numerous and very colourful, reddish, brown and yellowish, some to an inch (2·5 cm) long. Flowers are equally attractive, purplish pink, 2¼ in. (6 cm) long. Propagates easily from seeds.

T. lopothele is a Mexican species from Chihuahua, growing to a large globular plant of about 8 in. (20 cm) high, with a rather depressed crown. Ribs are slender, about 16, with very pronounced tubercles. Spines few, curved, yellowish, sometimes with one very long central spine. Flowers pale yellow on the inner surface, green with reddish stripes on the outer surface.

Fig. 15.
Thelocactus
bicolor.

Trichocereus (South America) (see also *Echinopsis*, p. 26)
A genus associated with tall growing plants—a generic title which will persist for a long time despite having been absorbed into *Echinopsis*. Many popular and well-known species are included, some of which make excellent grafting stock as young plants. All are of easy culture and stately habit, requiring full sun, ample moisture in the growing season and a long rest period. They make excellent greenhouse plants.

T. pasacana is endemic to Bolivia and Argentina, tall growing with about 25 very distinct ribs and areoles with long whitish yellow spines. Flower white, nocturnal.

T. macrogonus is an elegant, fast-growing species, the stem being rather bluish green with about 7 low rounded ribs and short brownish spines, and one longer to about an inch (2·5 cm) in length. Flowers are white and nocturnal.

46

Uebelmannia (Brazil)

A new genus created a few years ago for some of the most fascinating cacti yet brought into cultivation. All are globular or semi-cylindrical with peculiarities of body form which sets them aside as connoisseurs' plants. A rich porous soil should be provided, careful watering throughout the growing season and dry thereafter—minimum temperature of 10°C to 12°C (50°–55°F)—higher if possible for successful culture.

U. gummifera has a dull greenish body with many tubercled ribs, areoles with about 7 spines, the two central spines point one up, and one down. Flowers yellow.

U. pectinifera has dark reddish brown body entirely covered with whitish scales, giving the effect of being greyish blue. Ribs about 16, closely set with black pectinate spines, perpendicularly arranged, resembling a comb. Areoles in crown felted with greyish wool, from which small yellow flowers appear.

Weberocereus (Costa Rica, Panama)

A small genus of epiphytes, all slender stemmed with aerial roots, of either climbing or pendent habit. Require a moist, humid atmosphere, shaded from full sun, and temperature not less than 12°C (55°F). Suitable for an orchid-house climate.

W. biolleyi looks very much like a *Rhipsalis* in stem growth, slightly angled stems, night flowering with small rose-pinkish flowers. Native of Costa Rica.

Weingartia (South America)

A well-known group of globular plants, generally with turnip-shaped roots. They are probably closely linked to both *Gymnocalycium* and *Sulcorebutia*. Good greenhouse plants, free-flowering, requiring porous compost and only moderate watering at any time, dry in winter.

W. neocummingii is possibly synonymous with *W. cummingii*—there being little to differentiate between them. Bright green globular body, ribs divided into oval tubercles, woolly areoles with many whitish and brown spines. Flowers occur in a circle around the rather depressed crown, yellowish orange. Native of Peru.

W. fidaiana from Bolivia has an olive-green body, flattened tubercles and woolly areoles with 6–8 brown spines. Rather a small growing plant with orange-yellow flowers.

Werckleocereus (Guatemala, Costa Rica)

A true rain-forest epiphytic genus containing only two species. Both are of climbing habit with nocturnal flowers. Culture similar to *Weberocereus*, but less temperamental.

W. glaber, native of Guatemala, has 3-angled bright green stems, the margins having very distinct projections. Spines are few and small. Flowers are carried on a long spiney tube, about 4 in. (10 cm) long, pure white.

W. tonduzii develops a bushy appearance, stems 3–4 angled with straight margins and few spines. Flowers white on short dark spined tube. Costa Rica.

Wilcoxia (Mexico, U.S.A.)
Tuberous rooted plants with long, slender, erect stems and attractive colourful flowers. Suitable for greenhouse culture, these require a very porous soil, a little lime added can prove helpful. Careful watering is needed in warmest weather, although they should be kept completely dry in winter. Temperature 10°C (50°F).

W. schmollii has soft, slender, erect stems, about 10 tuberculate ribs with woolly areoles and small white thin spines. Flowers purplish rose with green stigma. Mexico.

W. poselgeri has very long and slender greyish green stems, minute spines and purplish pink flowers, the tube having many small spines and whitish hairs. Native to Texas and north Mexico.

Fig. 16. Mammillaria humboldtii.

48

Printed by Henry Stone & Son (Printers) Ltd., Swan Close, Banbury, Oxon.